Supporting Dyslexic Learners in the Secondary
Moira Thomson, MBE

DYSLEXIA:

ROLE OF THE TEACHING ASSISTANT

First published for schools in England in 2017 by CPD Bytes Ltd

ISBN 978-1-912146-34-5

This booklet is 1.10 in the series
Supporting Dyslexic Learners in the Secondary Curriculum (England)

Supporting Dyslexic Learners in the Secondary Curriculum   Moira Thomson, MBE

Complete set comprises 25 booklets

1.0   Dyslexia: Secondary Teachers' Guides

1.1   Identification and Assessment of Dyslexia at Secondary School

1.2   Dyslexia: Underpinning Skills for the Secondary Curriculum

1.3   Dyslexia: Reasonable Adjustments to Classroom Management

1.4   Dyslexia: Role of the Secondary School SENCo (Dyslexia Specialist Teacher)

1.5   Partnerships with Parents of Secondary School Students with Dyslexia

1.6   Dyslexia: ICT Support in the Secondary Curriculum

1.7   Dyslexia and Examinations (Reasonable Adjustments & Access Arrangements)

1.8   Dyslexia: Information for Guidance, Pastoral & Behaviour Support Teachers

1.9   Dyslexia: Learning Styles and Study Skills for the Secondary Curriculum

1.10   Dyslexia: Role of the Teaching Assistant

1.11   Dyslexia: Co-occurring & Overlapping Issues (Specific Learning Difficulties) NEW

2.0   Subject Teachers' Guides

2.1   Dyslexia: Art & Design Subjects

2.2   Dyslexia: Drama (Performing Arts; Theatre Studies)

2.3   Dyslexia: English (Communication)

2.4   Dyslexia: Home Economics (Child Development; Food & Nutrition)

2.5   Dyslexia: ICT Subjects (Business Subjects; Computer Science)

2.6   Dyslexia: Mathematics (Statistics)

2.7   Dyslexia: Modern Foreign Languages

2.8   Dyslexia: Music

2.9   Dyslexia: Physical Education (Sports; Games; Dance)

2.10   Dyslexia: Science Subjects (Biology; Chemistry; General Science; Physics)

2.11   Dyslexia: Social Subjects (Economics; Geography; History; Citizenship Studies;
         Philosophy; Religious Studies)

2.12   Dyslexia: The Classics (Classical Greek; Latin; Classical Civilisations) (2013)

2.13   Dyslexia: Media Studies NEW

2.14   Dyslexia: Social Sciences (Anthropology, Archaeology; Humanities; Psychology;
         Sociology) NEW

Foreword by Dr. Gavin Reid, formerly senior lecturer in the Department of Educational Studies, Moray House School of Education, University of Edinburgh. An experienced teacher, educational psychologist, university lecturer, researcher and author, he has made over 1000 conference and seminar presentations in more than 40 countries and has authored, co-authored and edited many books for teachers and parents.

ACKNOWLEDGEMENTS

Moira Thomson would like to thank the following for making possible the original publication of this important series of booklets:

- ✦ Dyslexia Scotland for supporting the publication and distribution of the original editions of these booklets
- ✦ The Royal Bank of Scotland for an education grant that funded Dyslexia Scotland's support
- ✦ Dr Gavin Reid for his encouragement over the years – and for writing the Foreword to these booklets
- ✦ Dr Jennie Guise of DysGuise Ltd for her support and professional advice
- ✦ The committee of Dyslexia Scotland South East for their support
- ✦ Alasdair Andrew for all his hard work and unfailing confidence
- ✦ Colleagues Maggie MacLardie and Janet Hodgson for helpful comments
- ✦ Cameron Halfpenny for proof reading and editing these booklets
- ✦ Current and former students, whose achievements make it all worthwhile

Moira Thomson MBE

2017

FOREWORD by Dr Gavin Reid

The Dyslexia booklets written by Moira Thomson have been widely circulated and highly appreciated by teachers throughout Scotland and beyond. I know they have also been used by teachers in a number of countries and this is testimony to the skills of Moira in putting together these booklets in the different subject areas of the secondary school curriculum.

It is therefore an additional privilege for me to be approached again by Moira to update this Foreword to the compendium of books developed by Moira in association with Dyslexia Scotland.

These updated guides are for all teachers - they contain information that will be directly relevant and directly impact on the practice of every teacher in every secondary school in the country. It is heartening to note that the guides again provide a very positive message to readers. The term Dyslexia is not exclusive to the challenges experienced by learners with dyslexia, but there is now a major thrust towards focussing on the strengths and particularly what they **can** do - and not what they 'can't do'. It is important to obtain a learning profile which can be shared with the student.

Moira encapsulates these points in these updated booklets. The focus is on supporting learners and helping them overcome the barriers to learning. At the same time it is important that learners with dyslexia, particularly in the secondary school develop responsibility for their own learning. The acquisition of self-sufficiency in learning and self-knowledge are important aspects of acquiring efficient learning skills for students with dyslexia. It is this that will stand them in good stead as they approach important examinations and the transition to tertiary education and the workplace. For that reason these guides are extremely important and need to be available to all teachers. Moira ought to be congratulated in endeavouring to achieve this.

The breadth of coverage in these guides is colossal. Moira Thomson has met this immense task with professionalism and clarity of expression and the comprehensiveness of the guides in covering the breadth of the curriculum is commendable.

As well as including all secondary school subjects the guides also provide information on the crucial aspects of supporting students preparing for examinations, the use of information and communication technology, information for parents, details of the assessment process and the skills that underpin learning. It is important to consider the view that learners with dyslexia are first and foremost 'learners' and therefore it is important that their learning skills are developed fully. It is too easy to place the emphasis on developing literacy skills at the expense of other important aspects of learning. The guides will reinforce this crucial point that the learning skills of all students with dyslexia can be developed to a high level.

The guides do more than provide information on dyslexia; they are a staff development resource and one that can enlighten and educate all teachers in secondary schools. I feel certain they will continue to be warmly appreciated. The guides have already been widely appreciated by teachers and school management as well as parents and other professionals but the real winners have been and will continue to be the **students** with dyslexia. It is they who will ultimately benefit and the guides will help them fulfil their potential and make learning a positive and successful school experience.

Dr Gavin Reid, April 2016

WHAT IS DYSLEXIA?

Dyslexia is widely recognised as a specific difficulty in learning to read.

Research shows that dyslexia may affect more than the ability to read, write and spell – and there is a growing body of research on these 'co-occurring' factors.

The Rose Report[1] identifies dyslexia as *'a developmental difficulty of language learning and cognition that primarily affects the skills involved in accurate and fluent word reading and spelling, characterised by difficulties in phonological awareness, verbal memory and verbal processing speed.'*

Dyslexia is a learning difficulty that primarily affects the skills involved in accurate and fluent word reading and spelling.

- Characteristic features of dyslexia are difficulties in phonological awareness, verbal memory and verbal processing speed.

- Dyslexia occurs across the range of intellectual abilities.

- It is best thought of as a continuum, not a distinct category, and there are no clear cut-off points.

- Co-occurring difficulties may be seen in aspects of language, motor co-ordination, mental calculation, concentration and personal organisation, but these are not, <u>by themselves,</u> markers of dyslexia.

- A good indication of the severity and persistence of dyslexic difficulties can be gained by examining how the individual responds or has responded to well founded intervention.

Rose Report page 10

Dyslexia exists in all cultures and across the range of abilities and socio-economic backgrounds. It is a hereditary, life-long, neuro-developmental condition. Unidentified, dyslexia is likely to result in low self-esteem, high stress, atypical behaviour, and low achievement.[2]

[1] Rose, J (2009)Identifying and Teaching Children and Young People with Dyslexia and Literacy Difficulties DCFS Publications - independent report to the Secretary of State for Children, Schools &Families June 2009. http://webarchive.nationalarchives.gov.uk/20130401151715/http://www.education.gov.uk/publications/eOrderingDownload/00659-2009DOM-EN.pdf

[2] From Scottish Government working definition of dyslexia http://www.gov.scot/Topics/Education/Schools/welfare/ASL/dyslexia [3] SEND Code of Practice 0-25 https://www.gov.uk/government/uploads/system/uploads/attachment_data/file/398815/SEND_Code_of_Practice_January_2015.pdf

Estimates of the prevalence of dyslexia vary according to the definition adopted but research suggests that dyslexia may significantly affect the literacy attainment of between 4% and 10% of children.

TEACHERS' RESPONSIBILITIES RE LEARNERS WITH DYSLEXIA

References: Part 6 of the Equality Act 2010; Part 3 of the Children and Families Act 2014

All children/young people are entitled to an appropriate education, one that is appropriate to their needs, promotes high standards and the fulfilment of potential - to enable them to:
- achieve their best
- become confident individuals living fulfilling lives, and
- make a successful transition into adulthood, whether into employment, further or higher education or training

SEND Code of Practice 0-25[3]

All schools have duties towards individual children and young people to identify and address their Special Educational Needs/Disability (SEND). Dyslexia that has a substantial, long-term, adverse impact on day-to-day learning may be both SEN and a disability.

Teachers' responsibilities for meeting the needs of dyslexic learners are the same as those for all students, and should include approaches that avoid unnecessary dependence on written text.

Teachers have a responsibility to provide a suitably differentiated subject curriculum, accessible to all learners, that provides each with the opportunity to develop and apply individual strengths – and to ensure that learners with SEND get the support they need to access this. Rose[4] suggests that all teachers should have 'core knowledge' of dyslexia characteristics – to help them to make adjustments to their practice that will prevent discrimination and substantial disadvantage.

The reasonable adjustments made by subject teachers in the classroom should be reflected in the arrangements made for examinations in the subject concerned.

For example – if a History teacher usually reads source materials aloud to the whole class – then - for dyslexic students in that class – the usual way of working with source materials is to have them read aloud. If a Science teacher usually permits a dyslexic student, who struggles with writing and spelling, to dictate - e.g. observations during an experiment - to a scribe or audio-recorder– this is evidence of the student's usual way of producing written work in that subject.

---

[3] SEND Code of Practice 0-25
https://www.gov.uk/government/uploads/system/uploads/attachment_data/file/398815/SEND_Code_of_Practice_January_2015.pdf
[4] Rose Report (2009) page 17

ROLE OF THE TEACHING ASSISTANT (TA)

TAs play a vital role in education and make a valuable contribution to the achievement and attainment of dyslexic students in the classroom on a daily basis – helping them to develop greater autonomy and reach higher academic standards – and to feel included in the whole school community – resulting in greater social awareness and improved self-esteem.

The increasing inclusion of students with SEND in mainstream schools over the years led to a greater demand for additional support for individual students in secondary subject classrooms - a demand often satisfied by the deployment of Teaching Assistants[5] - usually funded by the Pupil Premium.

The drive to raise standards in schools and tackle teacher workloads, the findings of the Deployment and Impact of Support Staff (DISS) Project[6] and the educational requirements of the 2010 Equality Act and the 2014 Code of Practice for SEND 0-25 - have all had an impact on the way TAs are now trained and deployed in schools.

The core duties of secondary school TAs may cover a range of whole school responsibilities – but they generally carry out a variety of functions to support teachers (and students) - though what they do varies between subject classes, key stages and even schools.

The TA role is to add value to what teachers do, not to replace them and deliver a filtered version of the subject curriculum to some students. TAs are not teachers and – no matter what their qualifications – they do not usually have the depth of subject knowledge that secondary teachers require – so adopting an informal 'teaching' role in a subject classroom is not an effective role for a TA. This may result in TA interactions with students in the context of the subject curriculum - compared to teachers' interactions with students – being reactive rather than proactive, and more concerned with the completion of tasks than with promoting students' learning and subject understanding.

In addition to technical and administrative support for subject teachers, TAs may provide specific support for individual students with SEND, as part of an Education, Health and Care (EHC) Plan or SEN Support Plan. Many deliver structured interventions to individuals or small groups and may be involved in pastoral/health care of students. The primary role of a TA working with dyslexic students may be the provision of individual support designed to:

- promote inclusion
- enable dyslexic students' access to the curriculum
- facilitate independent learning
- contribute to making Access exam arrangements

---

[5] The term Teaching Assistant (TA) is the most common job title used by schools when referring to support staff roles and is the term used in this booklet to refer to non-teachers who support the learning of dyslexic students.

[6] The DISS project - the largest study of teaching assistants and other school support staff carried out in the world, was conducted between 2003 and 2009. http://maximisingtas.co.uk/research/the-diss-project.php

DUTIES OF THE TA – TO PROMOTE INCLUSION (OF DYSLEXIC STUDENTS)

Schools organise provision for students with SEN and/or disabilities in different ways to suit their particular circumstances - and the functions associated with the TA role make an important contribution to improving outcomes for all students with SEND. The TA role is often crucial to the implementation of a school's SEN policy and TA input to meeting the needs of dyslexic students may be an essential element of the SEN support provision of individual schools and in the wider Local Offer.

In a secondary school, a TA's main objective may be to support subject teachers in providing access to high quality education for dyslexic students through involvement in the graduated approach to SEND (Assess – Plan – Do - Review)[7]. They may:

- draw a subject teacher's attention to possible dyslexic issues in the classroom
- carry out observations/administer tests as directed by the SENCo
- make positive contributions to planning meetings
- implement strategies in the SEN Support Plan (IEP[8])
- deliver specific interventions to support dyslexic students
- monitor student progress towards achieving outcomes in the SEN support plan
- evaluate the effectiveness of planned interventions for individual students

The TA - working in partnership with other team members, students, parents and other professionals to promote the inclusion of dyslexic students - will:

- interact appropriately and professionally with subject teachers and other colleagues and with students and parents/carers
- contribute to planning of joint actions within the SEND team
- refer matters beyond their competence/role to the SENCo or subject teacher
- implement school policies - having regard for students' home values and practices
- comply with parents' wishes – provided these do not conflict with school policies
- reassure parents who express concerns about their children
- ensure that parents' requests to see a teacher are dealt with promptly
- pass on concerns about students to the SENCo

A TA will promote the inclusion of dyslexic students by:

- establishing and maintaining relationships with individuals and groups to enhance dyslexic students' self-esteem, learning and achievement
- consulting, communicating and engaging with students, colleagues, and parents/carers, drawing on external sources of support and expertise as appropriate

---

[7] See Teaching Assistants' Graduated Approach to Dyslexia Support at the end of this booklet
[8] Individual Educational Plan – no longer a statutory requirement for SEND students

DUTIES OF THE TA – TO ENABLE ACCESS TO THE CURRICULUM (FOR DYSLEXIC STUDENTS)

Many students with dyslexia will be unable to perform within the secondary subject curriculum in the same way at the same rate as other students, as their dyslexia may impact not only literacy skills but also processing speed and working memory capacity. The role of the TA will be linked to the provision of interventions/strategies to compensate for these issues and to support dyslexic students' access to the curriculum at an appropriate level.

Provide literacy support to allow access to the curriculum
- Identify and deliver intervention strategies to support dyslexic students with literacy difficulties as directed by the SENCo/specialist dyslexia teacher

Assist in preparing the learning environment[9]
- Advise subject teacher re environmental issues affecting dyslexic learners – e.g. glare on whiteboard, background noise etc
- Prepare individualised resources and materials
- Identify learning materials for use appropriate to planned subject activities
- Confirm content and quality of materials with subject teacher

Contribute to planning of learning activities
- Be aware of the strengths and individual needs of dyslexic students
- Understand the most effective way in which to support the learning of individual dyslexic students for specific activities/tasks
- Discuss expected learning outcomes with teacher and agree upon success criteria
- Provide feedback for teacher on outcomes of learning activity

Support dyslexic students during learning activities
- Provide support for learning activities - e.g. repeat/rephrase teacher instructions
- Help assemble equipment – e.g. direct students to where this is stored
- Provide help with learning tasks – e.g. read text materials/activity directions aloud; set up computer work station
- Feed back to the teacher on progress made – and give details of individual support provided to help identify a dyslexic student's usual way of working

---

[9] See example of dyslexia friendly classroom organisation at the end of this booklet

DUTIES OF THE TA – TO FACILITATE INDEPENDENT LEARNING

A TA may promote independent learning by encouraging students to take responsibility for their own learning and promoting development of self-esteem.

Promote social and emotional development of students
- Support students in developing appropriate peer relationships
- Help to resolve issues between students amicably and with regard to school policies
- Employ strategies agreed by school via policies to raise self-esteem, such as using a rewards system and directed praise

Promote developing self-esteem of students through:
- Valuing individuals and their diversity
- Giving praise for effort and achievement in all areas
- Promoting individual strengths
- Creating opportunities for dyslexic students to experience success
- Supporting the provision of a low-stress learning environment

Contribute to health and wellbeing of students
- Be aware of strategies that help dyslexic students to settle into new settings
- Help students to adjust into new settings – e.g. introduce simple guides to help them find their way to subject classrooms (colour codes at tope/bottom of stairs etc)
- Recognise signs of distress and offer reassurance

Observe and report on student performance
- Knowledge of observation techniques and understanding types of reporting, including verbal and written
- Carrying out observations after consultation with the SENCo and subject teacher about purpose
- Record findings in agreed format

Support use of ICT in the classroom
- Be aware of the sorts of equipment available in school and where to find them
- Implement school procedures for reporting technical faults
- Ensure appropriate ICT equipment is available to dyslexic students for classroom use
- Check ICT equipment works and appropriate software is installed
- Support dyslexic students' use of ICT equipment and software classroom

Intervene to help students to develop literacy and numeracy skills
- Deliver structured interventions within a school's policies for literacy and numeracy
- Work with individuals and groups on structured programmes as directed by the SENCo or specialist dyslexia teacher

ROLE OF THE DYSLEXIA SPECIALIST TA

A TA often provides essential support for a school's specialist dyslexia teacher and many secondary TAs have undertaken additional training - and may have gained qualifications - in Specific Learning Difficulties/Dyslexia.

Planning

In the secondary curriculum, subject teachers may see a class only a few times a week, so they often take some time to get to know their students as individual learners. The targeted support in the subject classroom for students with dyslexia is often provided by a TA with experience and/or additional training in dyslexia. In order to have a positive impact on students' learning, subject teachers and TAs must work together to plan, deliver and evaluate their respective roles, responsibilities and contributions to lessons.

When this planning is not carried out, TAs often end up providing informal subject teaching to the lowest achieving group students, forced into a reactive role, according to student responses in the classroom, rather than being proactive to remove barriers to learning.

Strengths of TAs may lie, initially, in their knowledge of individual dyslexic students[10] and their awareness/experience of effective adjustments to classroom practice that can remove barriers to learning - being able to anticipate possible difficulties and plan adjustments to enable dyslexic students to access the subject curriculum and make progress towards the attainment of subject outcomes. However, TAs need to meet with subject staff to gain an understanding of key curriculum content and methodology in order to suggest and plan strategies then select interventions/approaches that build on dyslexic students' strengths and minimise their difficulties.

Some strategic planning should be done before the dyslexic students' first subject lesson.

Classroom Grouping

Learners with dyslexia have different strengths and areas of difficulty, so it is important that they are not placed in a 'dyslexic' group in a subject class to be taken by a TA. Nor should the TA be restricted to offering help only to targeted dyslexic students.

While 'dyslexia' grouping might appear to make it easier and quicker for dyslexic students to access TA help, all learners should have the opportunity to work with others of similar subject ability and the teacher in order to make progress in the curriculum and to become part of a peer group – not placed only in literacy-level groups working with the TA.

The TA's role in the subject classroom is not to act as an informal instructional resource for low-attaining students – but to monitor the activities of all groups so that - when a targeted individual with dyslexia meets a barrier to learning – relevant support may be offered.

---

[10] See example of a dyslexic student passport at the end of this booklet

Grouping for Structured Interventions

Sometimes, a subject teacher, the SENCo or dyslexia specialist teacher may group students with dyslexia together to work with a TA for a specific, structured intervention – e.g. to help develop reading[11] or keyboarding/handwriting skills.

In such cases, the TA should have been trained in the delivery of the intervention – which may even be 'scripted' to ensure consistency. Each student should be provided with materials at an appropriate ability/interest level – e.g. they do not all have to write the same story in order to develop the ability to e.g. write in sentences. Whether students are working on the same topic or writing different stories the TA can help each of them to develop strategies such as group discussion and mind mapping to help organise their thoughts and make it easier for their ideas to be written down.

Classroom Seating

No matter how the learners are grouped in the classroom, it is important that those with dyslexia who - e.g. have difficulty with glare on the whiteboard – are seated in the most advantageous position to minimise this.

It is not necessary for the TA to sit (or 'hover') beside a learner with dyslexia in order to provide support – a 'roving' role in the classroom is often more effective and makes it easier to spot a student who is 'stuck' and needs help and encouragement.

Learners with dyslexia are sometimes embarrassed about asking for help and sometimes feel that accepting this identifies them to others as being 'stupid' so the TA should make a point of offering some support to all learners at times. Some TAs arrange for dyslexic students to make unobtrusive signals that they need help – so any support offered by the TA appears to be unsolicited. This can help those whose self-esteem is so low that they might otherwise reject help and display disruptive or withdrawn behaviours when their dyslexia prevents them from completing classroom activities in the time allowed.

Preparing Lesson Materials

The TA should discuss any course activities that may raise barriers to learning for dyslexic learners with the subject teacher in advance of each lesson. Both will already be aware of the different needs of individuals, so some support may be prepared in advance – e.g. course materials may need to be adapted to enable those with dyslexia to make effective use of them. This task is often part of the TA's agreed duties – and most will be familiar with how to adapt - e.g. a topic worksheet - to make it more dyslexia friendly. For example:

- Enlarge the font and increase the line spacing
- Print on coloured paper – not just off-white but on pastel blue, green, yellow etc according to the known preferences of individual students

---

[11] See paired reading 'script' at the end of this booklet

- Create scaffolding materials e.g. a blank table for completion or provision of a list of key words
- Scan the material into the computer so that e.g. a text reader can be used
- Prepare an audio recording of content that an individual student can replay as often as needed

TA Instructional Role

The subject teacher and the TA may identify possible issues for dyslexic students as the lesson is discussed – resulting in some materials being produced in advance – e.g. a checklist for learners to follow or a flow chart illustrating the whole activity with arrows showing progression between steps. These resources could be issued in class by the teacher or the TA as individual students' needs arise.

However, every barrier to learning cannot be identified in advance, so the TA should anticipate dyslexic students' needs and plan for:
- creation of extra 'thinking time' to process information – dyslexics take more time than others to figure out what is required, so should not be pressed to complete tasks before they are ready
- repetition and/or re-wording of teacher instructions - making these short and simple – and repeating instructions one or two at a time
- the need to explain things several times, in a variety of ways - on a one-to-one basis in some cases
- checking students' understanding of instructions or questions by asking them to repeat these back
- not relying on verbal instruction alone – providing a variety of visual aids 'on demand' and demonstrating how to carry out some activities

Learning styles

Students with dyslexia can become successful learners - though their brains may process information differently - they may have very individual learning preferences that are not easily related to simple visual – auditory – kinaesthetic styles. While a multi-sensory teaching approach is often effective for dyslexic learners, the TA might explore what works for individual dyslexic students generally, and match this to the demands of the subject curriculum - then:
- Create opportunities for active learning e.g. purposeful movement around the room; verbalising data to help process it; visualising to aid working memory etc
- Allow more time than is usual for practice/rehearsal – dyslexic learners need to over-learn so may need to practice and repeat activities in lots of different ways to keep motivation and sustain interest
- Provide as much time as dyslexic students need to organise their thoughts and complete set work. Issue e.g. a pre-prepared story skeleton to help guide the flow of written work or arrange time after the lesson to finish a task

- Check that the level of text material to be used in a lesson is appropriate - read text material aloud to all students to help those who are dyslexic without singling them out; provide audio/digital versions of required subject reading for dyslexic students; pre-teach key words and subject-specific vocabulary in advance to dyslexic individuals
- Prepare scaffolding for note-taking – few dyslexic learners are able to listen and take notes at the same time - pre-teach dyslexic students who are unable to keep up with the dictation speed of the teacher how to e.g. write only key words under sub-headings
- Issue dyslexic students with copies of notes/information from the board - they can read these while others copy the material
- Show dyslexic students how to give written responses in key words or in note form and teach them how to expand these into longer sentences/paragraphs at a later time
- Teach the use of mind maps, charts, and diagrams/drawings etc as alternatives to extended writing where possible. Arrange with the teacher for these to be expanded later, if necessary
- Teach keyboard skills and provide daily practice to build up speed and accuracy (use 'games' approach software). Ensure that ICT is available for all writing activities

Self-esteem

TAs are usually aware that students with dyslexia often experience failure in simple everyday classroom activities and so may not expect to succeed at anything. However, dyslexics are often lateral and creative thinkers, full of originality - but are likely to need a lot of help to build their self-esteem. The TA might:
- ask dyslexic students how they learn best – what kinds of teaching approaches really work for them and what adjustments would help in the classroom – then suggest these methods to the subject teacher
- avoid asking any student – not only the dyslexics - to read aloud in a group unless they volunteer to do so
- always include positive comments when marking work – even if it is only *well done for spelling this word correctly today* - mark for content and not handwriting or spelling ability – avoid too many 'red' marks - list any corrections required on a separate page (at the back of the notebook).
- try to identify the strengths of a dyslexic individual and build on these

TAs should always be aware that dyslexic individuals think and learn in a different way and use dyslexic learners' own ideas of ways they can help themselves to process and remember. No matter how unusual these ways are, if that is how an individual learns THAT is the best way to support him or her!

ROLE OF THE TA IN DYSLEXIA FRIENDLY SCHOOL POLICY

A school's Dyslexia Policy may aim to:

- ensure that dyslexic students have the support required to access the curriculum
- facilitate and monitor progress of dyslexic students in the subject curriculum
- enable dyslexic students to achieve their full potential at secondary school

These aims may be achieved through the graduated approach to supporting individual students' access to the subject curriculum at an appropriate level – which includes TA support[12] in subject classrooms as part of the differentiated delivery of the curriculum. TA objectives might be to contribute to differentiation by:

- providing in-class support for individual students
- producing individualised curricular materials for students
- individualising tasks for specific students
- designing individual outcomes for students with dyslexia
- providing a range of teaching approaches to target individual learning preferences
- introducing technological support

Many of the duties of the TA as regards dyslexic students may have been developed through cooperative work with the SENCo/dyslexia specialist teacher, specifically:

- monitoring the implementation of the school's SEN/dyslexia policy
- contributing to the assessment of dyslexic students' learning needs – including carrying out structured observations in subject contexts[13]
- delivering support to individual students with dyslexia
- contributing to the reasonable adjustments made by teachers in subject classrooms
- supporting dyslexic students' access to the subject curriculum at an appropriate level
- helping establish dyslexic students' usual way of working for Access arrangements
- contributing to whole school staff training on dyslexia

In some schools, a dyslexia specialist HLTA[14] may work closely with the SENCo in:

- deploying and managing other TAs who work with dyslexic students
- administration of standardised tests as part of a dyslexia assessment
- making Access arrangements for dyslexic students in exams
- liaising with parents and external agencies

Where a school has undertaken the development of a 'dyslexia friendly' school policy, all TAs will be closely involved with both the SENCo and the dyslexia specialist teacher in the implementation of this across the curriculum.

---

[12] See example of a Dyslexia Friendly Classroom Organisation at the end of this booklet
[13] See example of Structured Observation Instrument at the end of this booklet
[14] Higher Level Teaching Assistant

ACCESS ARRANGMENTS FOR EXAMS – ROLE OF THE TA

Access arrangements are permitted only to ensure that exam candidates have an unhindered opportunity to demonstrate their subject knowledge and ability. If a dyslexic student is able to achieve the required outcomes of a course of study, but is unable to demonstrate this in the 'normal' way - then alternatives may be put in place. When there is a discrepancy between known subject ability and writing skills - a written test may prevent accurate assessment, so an Access arrangement – e.g. dictating to a scribe - is permitted.

Evidence of a candidate's need for access arrangements is assembled by the SENCo who is responsible for making application to the JCQ for Access arrangements. This will include:

- A recent assessment of dyslexia carried out by a specialist assessor
- Evidence from subject teachers that an individual student has greater difficulty than most of the other students in accessing the subject curriculum at an appropriate level without support.

Role of the TA

Subject teachers are asked to provide a 'picture of need' – but the TA may be best placed to contribute 'pen portraits' of dyslexic students to illustrate their 'usual way of working' by:

- listing relevant reasonable adjustments made in the classroom on a daily basis to prevent placing dyslexic students at a disadvantage compared to other students
- describing support and demonstrating that the quality/quantity of an individual student's work deteriorates considerably when this is not available

Reasonable adjustments for exams

The adjustments in a subject classroom may include 'dyslexia friendly' approaches that individual dyslexic students rely on to access the curriculum - such as:

- provision of extra time to compensate for a slow processing speed
- adapted course materials on different coloured paper or in enlarged format
- the use of coloured overlays
- use of a reading pen, a computer screen reader
- use of a word processor with spell-check for extended writing tasks
- frequent repetition of instructions for an activity aloud
- help from a reader when extra time allowances are not sufficient
- dictating to a voice recorder or a scribe to compensate for slow/illegible writing
- reminders/prompts to help focus concentration on a set task
- permission to verbalise or move about to help process responses

When the usual way of working is permitted as an Access arrangement, it is often a TA – known to the exam candidate - who will deliver this in the exam room.

FURTHER READING

Blatchford, P (2011) *Reassessing the Impact of Teaching Assistants: How Research Challenges Practice and Policy* Abingdon, Routledge

Bosanquet, P (2015) *The Teaching Assistant's Guide to Effective Interaction* Abingdon, Routledge - Sets out a role for teaching assistants that focuses on developing students' independence and ownership of learning and includes practical strategies and reflective activities to help TAs improve their support for students in everyday settings.

Burnham, L & Baker, B (2011) *Supporting Teaching and Learning in Schools (Secondary)* London, Heinemann

Cochrane, K & Saunders, K (Eds) (2012) *Dyslexia Friendly Schools Good Practice Guide* Bracknell, British Dyslexia Association

Hull City Council (2016) *Supporting Children with Dyslexia* London, David Fulton/NASEN Revised and updated in light of the 2014 SEND Code of Practice, this 2nd edition provides advice and resources for teachers, TAs and SENCos supporting learners with dyslexia.

MacKay, N (2005) *Removing Dyslexia as a Barrier to Achievement: The Dyslexia Friendly Schools Toolkit* 3rd Edition (2012) Wakefield, SEN Marketing - Full of practical guidance, empowering ideas and challenging assertions about inclusion, presenting strategies for meeting diverse learning needs and overcoming barriers to learning.

Mortimore, T (2008) *Dyslexia and Learning Style: A Practitioner's Handbook* 2nd Edition Chichester, John Wiley & Sons

Reid, G & Green, S (2007) *The Teaching Assistant's Guide to Dyslexia* London, Continuum This practical guide gives the TA useful advice on:
- Understanding and identifying dyslexia
- Developing effective strategies for aiding the learning of dyslexic pupils
- Supporting different learning styles through the development of study skills
- Encouraging self-esteem

Thomson, M (2007) *Supporting Students with Dyslexia at Secondary School – every class teacher's guide to removing barriers and raising attainment* Abingdon, Routledge - Focuses on the teaching and learning of students with dyslexia in the context of the mainstream secondary curriculum. Provides practical guidance by highlighting barriers to learning experienced by dyslexic learners in today's curriculum and advice for removing – or minimising – these barriers

Thurtle, S (2012) *Dyslexia in Education: a guide for teachers and teaching assistants* Bracknell, BDA - How to recognise dyslexia and likely strengths and weaknesses – and offers practical ideas for supporting students and building self-esteem in the mainstream classroom.

DYSLEXIA INDICATORS AT THE SECONDARY STAGE (PHOTOCOPIABLE)

Dyslexia is more than an isolated defect in reading or spelling. The problem may be perceptual, auditory receptive, memory-based or a processing deficit.

Subject teachers are not expected to be able to diagnose these difficulties as such, but some general indications are listed below. If several of these are observed frequently in the classroom, subject teachers should tick the relevant boxes to identify issues when referring a student for further investigation.

Student Name: _____ Class: _____ Date: _____

- ☐ Quality of written work does not adequately reflect the known ability of the student in the subject

- ☐ Good orally but very little written work is produced – many incomplete assignments

- ☐ Disappointing performance in timed tests and other assessments

- ☐ Poor presentation of work – e.g. illegibility, mixed upper and lower case, unequal spacing, copying errors, misaligned columns (especially in Maths)

- ☐ Poor organisational skills – the student is unable to organise self or work efficiently; carries either all books or wrong ones; frequently forgets to hand in work

- ☐ Sequencing poor – student appears to jump from one theme to another, apparently for no reason

- ☐ Inability to memorise (especially in Maths and Modern Languages) even after repeated practice

- ☐ Inability to hold numbers in short-term memory while performing calculations

- ☐ Symbol and shape confusion (especially in Maths)

- ☐ Complains of headaches when reading; sometimes sees patterns/distortions in printed text; says that words move around the page or that text is glaring at them

- ☐ Unable to carry out operations one day which were previously done adequately

- ☐ Unable to take in and carry out more than one instruction at a time

- ☐ Poor depth perception – e.g. clumsy and uncoordinated, bumps into things, difficulty judging distance, catching balls, etc

- ☐ Poor self-image – lacking in confidence, fear of new situations – may erase large quantities of written work, which is acceptable to the teacher

- ❑ Tires quickly and work seems to be a disproportionate return for the effort involved in producing it

- ❑ Easily distracted – either hyperactive or daydreaming

- ❑ **Other – details below**

Teacher: _____ Subject: _____

Action/information requested:

- ❑ details of known SEND and support required

- ❑ investigation of SEND and advice on graduated support

- ❑ dyslexia assessment

- ❑ profile of learning needs

- ❑ suggest reasonable adjustments to be made in class

- ❑ suggest learning objectives and outcomes for SEN plan

- ❑ advice re Access arrangements

TEACHING ASSISTANTS' GRADUATED APPROACH TO DYSLEXIA SUPPORT

All TAs should have 'core knowledge' of dyslexia characteristics – to help them to offer appropriate support and make adjustments to prevent discrimination and substantial disadvantage in the classroom, including:

- Recognition of the range and diversity of the learning preferences and styles of individual dyslexic learners

- Awareness of the learning differences related to dyslexia that may cause difficulties within the subject curriculum
    - Acknowledgement of the very severe literacy difficulties some dyslexic learners experience
    - Understanding that some dyslexic students - who seem to have only minor problems with literacy - may experience difficulties with higher order skills, especially working memory and processing speed in subject classes

- Making adjustments to appropriate, differentiated teaching and learning materials so they are more easily accessible by dyslexic students

- Commitment to the need to reduce barriers to learning linked to the delivery of the curriculum as well as those due to the impact of dyslexia

- Provision of individual support for some learners with dyslexia within the context of a subject and consultation with parents, subject teachers and the SENCo/specialist dyslexia teacher (and the young person) to determine how best to provide this

- Willingness to ask for advice and support from the SENCo and/or dyslexia specialist teacher if a dyslexic learner does not make progress towards achieving subject outcomes

- Understanding that, while dyslexia is not linked to ability, able dyslexic learners may persistently underachieve or appear to lack interest in a subject

- Knowledge that many dyslexic learners use strategies such as misbehaviour or illness for coping with difficulties they do not necessarily understand themselves

- Taking account of the difficulties experienced by dyslexic learners when monitoring progress – identifying reasonable adjustments for assessments (Access Arrangements) that reflect the additional support usually provided in the classroom

Dyslexic learners constantly meet barriers to learning across the curriculum and may become discouraged very quickly due to lack of initial success in subject classes. This may result in subject teachers and TAs assuming that they are inattentive or lazy, when they are actually working much harder than their classmates, but with little apparent effect.

EXAMPLE OF A STRUCTURED (SCRIPTED) INTERVENTION - PAIRED READING

Studies indicate that regular paired reading leads to an increase in reading accuracy, fluency, and expression. Research indicates that children find the method described below easy to use, and feel they are more competent readers as a result of paired reading.[15]

Paired reading partners may be parents - or other students – but many schools include this activity in the structured interventions provided by TAs. Paired reading sessions might take place on a daily basis, each lasting for about 10 - 20 minutes.

Preparation for Reading
- Student and TA meet to talk about reading issues and plan their sessions
- They identify what they will read and set objectives – e.g. to meet the demands of the KS3 English curriculum
- They arrange a timetable of reading sessions
- A quiet location should be identified for reading sessions, away from visual distractions and background noise

At the first Reading Session
- Student chooses reading materials (and can change them at any time)
- They agree on a 'starting signal'
- They begin reading aloud together
- TA comments on any issues identified during the session

Reading Together
- Always begin by reading together
- If an error is made, the TA says the word, and the student repeats it – without comment

Reading Alone
- Student and TA identify a signal for reading alone
- TA praises the student when reading alone is signalled
- TA continues to offer support and praise while the student is reading alone

Return to Paired Reading (until the student decides to read alone again)
- TA corrects any student mistake (gives word, and student repeats it)

'Post-mortem' Talk
- At the end of the session, relax and talk about what has been read and the student is encouraged to express an opinion

---

[15] See **Topping, K** (1995) *Paired Reading, Spelling and Writing: The Handbook for Teachers and Parents,* Continuum Publications, London, UK

EXAMPLE OF A DYSLEXIC STUDENT 'PASSPORT'

Name: _____ Year _____ Class _____

About me: _____

Photograph	_____
	_____
	_____
	_____

My strengths

I am good at sports and drama and making friends
I am confident in using a computer and a calculator
I usually manage to keep up with the class in lessons (except writing)

I want you to know that

I am a slow reader – but with enough time, I understand what I read.
I am not good at copying things from the board – sometimes I can't see this very well and I miss bits out
My spelling is not good, but I can use a computer spell checker

I am working on

Developing faster keyboarding so I can use a computer to help with writing
Improving my reading speed
Remembering to bring the correct books and equipment every day

How you can help me

Warn me in advance of questions I need to answer
Give me time to think of an answer and write it down
Don't give me more than 2 instructions at a time – I forget them
Check I have written the homework down correctly

EXAMPLE OF DYSLEXIA – FRIENDLY CLASSROOM ORGANISATION

TAs might help subject teachers to minimise barriers to learning in their classrooms by arranging/supporting the following adjustments:

- Review classroom lighting – check for glare from sunlight/class lighting on white boards and identify the most favourable seating for dyslexic students
- Suggest an acceptable level of student movement during a lesson without being disruptive – help create a classroom rule specifying this

- Identify opportunities in subject context for collaborative learning and peer support - 'study buddies' - for dyslexic students – provide 'training' in this activity for all student buddies – monitor level of talk and work rate in class
- Create alternatives to copying from the board – compile skeleton notes to be annotated or provide full copies for dyslexic students to read while others copy
- When the whiteboard is interactive, send notes directly to dyslexic students' laptops or to a prearranged folder on the school intranet for them to download
- If notes are dictated – record these – and help dyslexic students to store these as voice files or transcribe them and issue print versions
- Print subject materials on non-white paper (e.g. cream – or a colour specified by an individual dyslexic student) using an accessible font/line spacing/layout
- Identify key words in texts to dyslexic students to help reading comprehension
- Ensure all classroom resources are clearly labelled
- Provide ICT/technological support in the classroom - demonstrate how and when to:
  - use electronic dictionaries/spell checkers/reading pens
  - adjust computer screen resolution and background colour
  - change text size/colour/font/line spacing
  - access dyslexia support software on tablet/laptop
  - use software to support reading and spelling effectively
  - use a digital voice recorder to make personal notes or record teacher
  - use the camera on a tablet or phone to copy/save information
- Arrange the provision of easily accessible classroom resources/materials for dyslexic students – encourage students to use these without interrupting a lesson to ask permission – e.g.:
  - Highlighter pens/post-it pads
  - computer screen filters
  - tinted 'reading rulers'
  - templates/blank tables for completion
  - key words spelling list
  - electronic dictionaries, calculators, reading pens etc.

EXAMPLE OF A CLASSROOM OBSERVATION RECORD (PHOTOCOPIABLE)[16]

Pupil: _____   Date: _____

Subject: _____   Time of day: _____

Note content, teaching strategies used, differentiation, resources etc.

Description of main lesson activity: (circle) *practical /reading/writing/listening/copying*

Scan and record student learning behaviour at approximately 20 second intervals.

Dyslexia Indicator	Frequency observed
poor auditory discrimination	
asks what was said (page number etc)	
can't remember instructions	
appears not to hear teacher's talk	
poor visual discrimination	
complains can't see (e.g. the board)	
squints at text, moves book a lot	
difficulties copying	
asks others what text says	
difficulty organising work & desk	
appears not to try to start work	
does not write continuously	
writes very little	
often asks how to spell words	
avoidance strategies (e.g. ill, no pencil)	
tires quickly, takes rests/breaks	
does not volunteer answers	
refuses to read aloud	
gets angry when struggling with task	

Comment on:

Settling down to work:

Following instructions: Written   Spoken

Asking for help: **Teacher interventions:**

Co-operation with others: **Completion of set tasks:**